The Disappearance of Dorothy Arnold: The Unsolved Mystery of the American Socialite Who Vanished in 1910

By Charles River Editors

Dorothy Arnold

About Charles River Editors

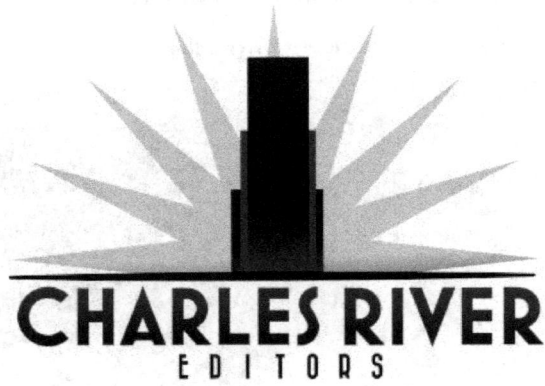

Charles River Editors is a boutique digital publishing company, specializing in bringing history back to life with educational and engaging books on a wide range of topics. Keep up to date with our new and free offerings with this 5 second sign up on our weekly mailing list, and visit Our Kindle Author Page to see other recently published Kindle titles.

We make these books for you and always want to know our readers' opinions, so we encourage you to leave reviews and look forward to publishing new and exciting titles each week.

Introduction

The Disappearance of Dorothy Arnold (1910)

It was the great mystery of its time and still reads like an episode of "Law and Order" today. In December 1910, a wealthy young woman, thought to be sheltered and above reproach, goes missing shortly after being seen in broad daylight on Fifth Avenue in New York City. The police are called in and begin to question those closest to her, only to have her father, a wealthy manufacturer, insist it must be foul play and that his daughter was on good terms with her entire family. Likewise, he claims that though she was in her mid-20s and in the prime of life, she had no serious romantic attachments. The mother tearfully backs these claims up.

Eventually, far different information leaks out, like the fact that the victim was an aspiring writer who kept much about her work a secret, that she had been trying to cut ties with her family for some time, and, most interesting of all, that there certainly was a boyfriend, and that her family had tried to hide their relationship. For a time, all eyes are on the romantic interest, who is significantly older but a longtime friend of the family. In fact, the victim's brother is seen in beautiful Florence, Italy, beating the boyfriend up in a failed attempt to get more information about his sister's disappearance. Letters surface, as do photographs, but ultimately nothing to indicate the he had anything at all to do with her disappearance. Finally, everyone gives up and turns their attentions elsewhere.

Meanwhile, there are rumored sightings, as she is "seen" in various large cities across the United States and Europe. Mentally ill women claim to be her, but again and again, no lead checks out. Eventually, the story grows cold and people lose interest, but then, more than three years after she disappeared, a new lead turns up. A back room abortionist claims that she came to him for an "illegal" operation and died, and as he did with all his other victims, he cremated her body and tossed out the ashes. The story makes the front pages for days, even as the family denies it is possible, but by now, it's April 1914 and the newspapers have more pressing matters to report, so the story quickly falls off their radar again.

While the story was certainly fit for a gripping thriller, it was all too true for Dorothy Arnold and her family. Arnold was a young, well-known socialite whose disappearance was front page news on the East Coast in the early 20th century, and over 100 years later, armchair gumshoes continue trying to piece together the puzzle over her fate. In an era before other famous disappearances like that of the Lindbergh baby and Jimmy Hoffa became grist for writers, it was Dorothy Arnold who left people wondering and speculating. To this day, the mystery remains unsolved and, except for periodic stories and lists about enduring mysteries, largely forgotten.

The Disappearance of Dorothy Arnold: The Unsolved Mystery of the American Socialite Who Vanished in 1910 looks at one of the early 20th century's most enduring mysteries. Along with pictures of important people, places, and events, you will learn about the disappearance of Dorothy Arnold like never before.

The Disappearance of Dorothy Arnold: The Unsolved Mystery of the American Socialite Who Vanished in 1910

About Charles River Editors

Introduction

    Chapter 1: Before the Disappearance

    Chapter 2: Arnold's Disappearance

    Chapter 3: Alive or Dead?

    Chapter 4: New Searches and New Theories

    Chapter 5: Subsequent Sightings, Stories, and Hoaxes

    Online Resources

    Bibliography

Free Books by Charles River Editors

Discounted Books by Charles River Editors

Chapter 1: Before the Disappearance

Pictures of Dorothy Arnold

In 1960, author Allen Churchill wrote of a nearly forgotten story: "The total mystery of the Dorothy Arnold case is as unfathomable today as it was fifty years ago. Dorothy Arnold was hardly the madcap, kick-up-her-heels type of girl who might easily get into trouble. One had simply to look at her wide, placid lace to realize that she was more studious than frivolous. She had graduated from Bryn Mawr five years before and still retained the serene, slightly lofty demeanor of the ultra serious female collegian. A quiet-looking, sturdy girl with a healthy complexion, she had brown hair done up in a high pompadour, and steady, blue-gray eyes. By modern standards, the Arnold family would seem stuffy and somewhat forbidding. It was presided over by chop-whiskered Francis R. Arnold, a seventy-three year-old businessman, who proudly traced his lineage straight back to the Mayflower; it was his sister who had married Supreme Court Justice Rufus Peckham. Mrs. Arnold was equally well-connected, and the family ranked high in the old guard of New York society, then noted for its propriety and unbending reticence. On the day of her disappearance, Dorothy Arnold was expensively and modishly clad, a fact that would make her highly conspicuous at a time when class distinctions in female dress were sharp. That day she wore a well-tailored suit, with a blue serge coat and a tight hobble skirt in a matching color; she carried both a huge silver-fox mutt and a satin handbag. But by far the most conspicuous feature of her attire was her hat. It was made of black velvet, with two blue roses for decoration—a type then called a 'Baker,' which resembles nothing so much as an overturned dishpan. The lining of this oversized chapeau was Alice blue, the maker's name was 'Genevieve,' and along its edge, rimming Dorothy's pleasant, open face, ran a fetching bit of scalloped lace."

Rufus Peckham

In fact, prior to her disappearance, Arnold had lived her entire life in a more or less uneventful manner, with her name only appearing in an occasional social column. She was born on July 1, 1886 in New York City and named Dorothy Harriet Camille Arnold. She and her three siblings were raised by a staff of nannies and sent to the Veltin Day School for Girls on 160-162 West 74th Street in Manhattan. There, in addition to other standard subjects, she learned to speak French.

Upon graduation, her parents enrolled her in Bryn Mawr to study literature. She graduated from the school in 1905 determined to be a writer and moved back into her parents' East 79th Street home while she pursued her efforts.

After years of writing various pieces, in 1910 Arnold finally submitted a story to *McClure's* magazine, but after having gotten most things she wanted in life, she was shocked when they rejected her story. To make matters worse, her family and friends failed to take her efforts seriously, and they teased her good naturedly about her failure. Offended and no doubt embarrassed, Dorothy vowed to never tell them anything else about her efforts until she was published, going so far as to rent a post office box in her own name, a move that would only come to light after her disappearance when a newspaper reported, "Miss Arnold…was sensitive about her failure to get her work published, and had been twitted on the subject by her brother, Jack. So, to keep the family from knowing of her repeated failures to get stories accepted, she dealt with the magazines through the general delivery."

McClure's, some years before it rejected Arnold's story

Chapter 2: Arnold's Disappearance

A New York Tribune picture of Arnold in 1910

In October 1910, Dorothy approached her father about moving out on her own, telling him she felt she would be more successful in Greenwich Village as opposed to the family's stuffy home on 79th Street. Though she was in her mid-20s, Francis Arnold forbade her to live on her own and, in answer to her pleas, declared that a good writer could write anywhere. The unspoken rebuke stung, especially when another one of Arnold's stories was rejected in November, just weeks before she disappeared. One can only wonder if his harsh words to his daughter contributed to his subsequent grief, which was immense, at least according to one account following his daughter's disappearance in the New York *Post*: "Miss Arnold's father, who is 73 years old, is almost prostrated with grief and worry, and his wife also is on the verge of nervous collapse. They say they will give any reasonable reward for information leading to the discovery of the daughter. Miss Arnold has lived in New York all her life and has many friends here. For that reason her family shrank from the publicity that an open search would entail, but her parents are so overcome by their failure to find the slightest that they seized upon the newspapers as the last hope of finding her."

Within a day of Dorothy's disappearance on December 12, 1910, the first stories began to appear, and they filled in the blanks regarding her activities on the day she went missing. According to an initial report, "On the morning [of December 12], Miss Arnold told her mother that she was going to a Fifth avenue shop to buy an evening gown. 'I'll go with you,' her mother told her. 'No,' replied Miss Arnold, 'when I find a dress that I like I'll telephone you.' Miss Arnold left her home at about 11:30 a. m. Shortly after 12 o'clock, as' the family have since learned, Miss Arnold went to Park & Tilford's store in Fifth avenue, near Fifty-ninth street, and bought a half-pound box of candy. Between 1:30 and 2 o'clock she was in Brentano's store and purchased a current novel. This was learned when the bills for the novel and the candy came to Mr. Arnold. All the work of the army of detectives to get further trace of Miss Arnold after she left the stores has been fruitless...After following up every possible line in their search for the young woman, the detectives were forced to admit tonight that she either became mentally unbalanced without the slightest warning and wandered away or else she met with foul play. The detectives declared there was not the slightest step that could be taken in search for a missing person that they have not already taken. Search was made for the young woman in Washington and Boston as well as in New York. The facts of the young woman's disappearance were made public by former Assistant District Attorney Francis P. Garvan and John H. Keith, who is in his law firm, at Mr. Garvan's home. Mr. Garvan declared that he was discussing the case frankly and concealing nothing."

Not surprisingly, the story of the missing girl made its way quickly through both formal and informal circles, and friends began to come forward to tell their often hushed up stories. Writer Allen Churchill discussed some of them in 1960, "Return now to the Arnold home. Never had Dorothy skipped a meal without warning the family ahead of time. When she failed to return for dinner, an increasingly worried group ate without her, then began making discreet phone calls to Dorothy's close friends to ask if the girl had, by any chance, dropped in on them. Told that she had not, the Arnolds begged that no mention ever be made of their call. That night Elsie Henry, one of the girl friends queried, called back shortly after midnight to ask if Dorothy had returned. Mrs. Arnold answered the phone and committed the first of several acts that caused many to believe that the family knew more than it ever let on about Dorothy's disappearance. 'Yes, she's here,' Mrs. Arnold stated brightly, in reply to Elsie Henry's question. But when Elsie asked to speak to Dorothy there was a momentary silence. 'Oh, she had a headache and went right to bed,' Mrs. Arnold finally replied. Over breakfast the next morning, a distracted family settled on another strange move when they decided not to summon police, instead, Dorothy's brother John phoned a friend named John S. Keith, a junior partner in the law firm of Garvan K. Armstrong. Only a year or two older than Dorothy, Keith had occasionally escorted her to society dances or to lectures at the Metropolitan Museum of Art. Young Arnold asked Keith to stop at the house on his way downtown that morning. Keith was reluctant to do so. 'Can't it wait?' he asked. 'No, this is serious,' John Arnold replied."

It was only on the morning of January 25, 1911, over a month after Arnold's disappearance, that subscribers to the *Washington Post* awoke to some startling news. "Dorothy H. C. Arnold, a graduate of Bryn Mawr College in the class of 1905, and a daughter of Francis R. Arnold, an importer of perfumes, left her home on the forenoon of December 13 last to buy an evening gown. She has not been heard from since, although Deputy Police Commissioner Flynn's best men and private detectives have been following up every possible clew. Every precaution has been taken to keep Miss Arnold's disappearance secret up to tonight, although Mr. Arnold was advised some time ago that if it were made public in the newspapers there was a possibility that avenues would be reached which have not yet been covered. Mr. Arnold at last consented to give the facts to the newspapers tonight…Miss Arnold is a niece of the late Justice Peckham, of the United States Supreme Court, her father being a brother of Mrs. Peckham. Miss Arnold's aunt, Mia Peckham, widow of the justice, is dying at her home in Washington, partly, it is believed, as the result of worry over the strange disappearance of the niece. … She is one of the four children and is next to the oldest. John W. Arnold, her brother, is 26 and she is 25 years old. Another brother, D. Hinckley, is 20, and her only Sister, Marjorie, is 18. She has lived at home since she was graduated from Bryn Mawr, and has devoted most of her time to reading."

Many of those reading the article were shocked and rushed to their telephones or hurried off to send telegrams of condolence and encouragement to the Arnold family, and as the news made its way up and down the East Coast, newspapers published more details about her disappearance. According to the January 27th edition of the *Washington Post*, "Francis R. Arnold, the perfumery importer, will pay $1,000 to anybody who can furnish any useful information as to the movements of his daughter after she walked out of Brentano's on the afternoon of December 12, with a copy of Emily Calvin Blake's 'An Engaged Girl's Sketches' under her arm. That is the last verified news her family and friends have of her, although private detectives have searched every large city in the East, European steamship ports, and carried on for 45 days an extraordinarily painstaking and detailed investigation. Forty-five days ago, at 1:30 p. m., she walked up Fifth avenue, carrying a box of candy and a new book of fiction, and the New York police, the detective agencies, and hundreds of friends working quietly have not been able to follow her a step further. She had only about $30 with her at the time. it was a young woman friend who greeted her casually as she came out of Brentano's, and turned north along the avenue. The girl paused for a moment. 'You're looking well, Dorothy,' she' said. 'I'm feeling fine,' said Miss Arnold. 'I'm going to walk home through Central park.' She…frequently Strolled through the park on her way home from shopping or lunching at Sherry's or matinees. Absolutely…unable to explain why a girl who lived happily at home, had all the money she wanted, took pleasure in the society of Bryn Mawr schoolmates, enjoyed the theaters and her books, and appeared to be normal in every way, should deliberately turn her back on home and friends, the Arnolds insist that either she has been kidnapped or injured or has lost her senses."

In fact, those three explanations, all built around the idea that Arnold would not have disappeared of her own volition, remained the only theories that her family would entertain. Not wanting to work through the police, the Arnold's hired detectives from the famous Pinkerton Agency to try to track down their daughter. There were also two police detectives assigned to the case, but they were not emotionally involved with its outcome and thus had different ideas about what might have happed. As the January 27th edition of the *Washington Post* noted, "in the first few days of the search, it occurred to Francis P. Garvan and John H. Keith, who were consulted at once by Mr. Arnold, that the purchase of candy and a book indicated a premeditated intention to leave home. She might have got them to entertain herself on a railroad trip. Plenty of girls buy sweetmeats and novels while out shopping, but they go home. Here was a girl who did not, so they began the tedious business of questioning railroad ticket sellers, train conductors, and chair car porters, and in the course of a few days they had talked to ticket sellers of all the roads leading to big cities in the East, and had questioned closely hundreds of trainmen. Nobody remembered having seen a girl of Dorothy Arnold's description. For this reason and because she had not made the least preparation for even a short trip from home, the family assured themselves that she had not-gone voluntarily. They knew that she was to be the hostess at home on the afternoon of Thursday, December 17, at a tea party for 60 Bryn Mawr girls. The invitations had been sent out and all arrangements had been made for the party."

The plans for a party 5 days after Arnold's disappearance certainly raised questions. After all, why would a young woman planning to leave town for a long trip, or perhaps forever, devote her last few days at home to planning a party she had no intention of attending? Moreover, as the article pointed out, "She was on jolly terms with so many of her college friends that nobody in the family could imagine her leaving without whispering the secret to at least one or two of them. But she did not communicate with any one of them and many of the girls have been helping the family in the search. Her room disclosed no evidences of premeditated flight. She left behind most of her jewelry, all of the pieces on which she could have obtained much money. Of the fur set she was fondest of wearing—a muff and stole of black fox—she took only the muff and left the stole in her wardrobe. And what seemed most important to the family, she neither removed nor attempted to destroy a considerable mass of private correspondence—letters and notes and telegrams"

These facts raised further questions, most notably the question of why someone so unhappy with her family life that she was going to sneak away would leave behind personal, and even intimate, correspondence. It would have been easy to conceal such items in a handbag or to burn them, but instead they were left behind, allowing the article to describe some of their contents: "These were most carefully scrutinized and they gave the story of only one love affair. There were letters from a man whose admiration was plainly evident and who, so far as could be inferred from his own letters, believed that his love was reciprocated in part at least."

With that information coming to light, the theory that Arnold had eloped arose. The article explained, "The investigation took a new road here. The man who had written affectionately was in Europe when the girl disappeared. He is still there. The family know him quite well and creditably, but they were disregarding no apparent [clues]. Private detectives watched his house in this city Private detectives observed him in one or two European capitals. It was thought necessary to intercept letters coming to him here and abroad. The letters were intercepted and read. He did not make a movement abroad that was not reported to the Arnold family. it was unnecessary, as events showed. After weeks of espionage the Arnolds decided to approach the man directly and ask him if he knew where Dorothy was or if he had any notion that she intended to leave home. He satisfied the family and Mr. Garvan and Mr. Keith as well that he was as much mystified as they. Since then he has not been under observation. The family are convinced that it was not because of that love affair that she is missing. Was there any other romance in her life that might have led to unhappiness and flight? Mr. Arnold did not think so. His wife and his other daughter, Marjorie, who is 18 years old, had never heard Dorothy, mention any man particularly, nor did she act as if she had a love affair. Up to the day of her disappearance she led, they say, her usual placid life, and seemed to have no troubles more serious than a grievance against a dressmaker. it was possible, as Mr. Garvan and Mr. Keith said, that Dorothy knew a number of young men, but they did not think she was in love with any of them. Her girl friends told the family that they had never seen her about with any young man in particular, and that they would have known of it, very likely, if she had been in love."

The story continued to make front page news over the next few days, and on January 30, the *Washington Post* carried a special report from New York that began with a startling piece of news: "it was learned today from Herbert J. Carroll, a young man, who is in charge of the steamship department of Raymond & Whitcomb, dealers in transportation, next door to Brentano's and in the same building, that he had given information about West Indian sailings one day early in December to a young woman who closely resembled Dorothy Arnold. He thought, although he was not positive, that he talked to this young woman on the afternoon of December 12. The police do not think there is a single indication that Dorothy came to harm in Central park. The second deputy, Mr. Flynn, who convinced himself nearly two weeks ago that the investigation was hardly a reasonable field for police work, said today that he has seen no reason to change his opinion. 'I have concluded,' said Commissioner Flynn, 'that Miss Arnold is unharmed, and will come home when she feels like it. I cannot discuss the case further, because I was made the confident of the family, and am bound by that confidence.' While nothing more of a dependable nature has developed to explain why Miss Arnold left home or where she is now, all that has been discovered appears to show that she disappeared of her own volition."

Chapter 3: Alive or Dead?

By the end of January 1911, the entire police department considered the case closed, as the *Washington Post* noted on January 30: "The detective bureau dropped the case because its officials became satisfied that the girl left home because she wanted to, and that she had a right, being of age, to do as she pleased. The detectives were aware of all that John S. Keith, the Arnold family lawyer, has been led to admit piecemeal in the last few days."

In fact, it seems Keith had been rather loose lipped with a number of details that the family might just as soon have kept quiet. According to the same article, "They knew, for instance, that she was not going toward the park, but away from it, when she bought candy at Park & Tillford's; that she had been corresponding clandestinely with some person or persons in Europe; that the Arnolds had sent John W. Arnold, Dorothy's brother, to Florence to have a talk with George S. Griscom, Jr., the Pittsburgher, who was the most frequent caller at the Arnold home last summer, and they satisfied themselves that they withheld certain facts. in this connection the American today printed the following: 'Mrs. Francis R. Arnold, mother of Dorothy Arnold, is believed to be with her daughter. That she went to the missing girl after getting word from her appears to be almost certain.' These pertinent conclusions have forced themselves upon those who have been investigating the strange disappearance of Miss Arnold. That the girl's mother left home after her daughter's disappearance, and that her going away is connected with the case of her daughter, is conceded. To all concerned the vanishing of Mrs. Arnold is as deep a mystery as the disappearance of her daughter. John S. Keith told the American yesterday that Mrs. Arnold left home 'some time after the holidays.' Pressed to reveal the exact time Mr. Keith reflected and said 'that it was shortly after January 1. It might have been a day or so after New Year's day.' John W. Arnold, brother of Miss Arnold, it was admitted by Mr. Keith, started abroad on January 3."

Writing decades later, Allen Churchill described the presumed love interest who private investigators were tailing across Europe: "He was hardly the type to sweep a girl off her feet, or rescue her from a stifling existence. Instead, he seemed desperately in need of rescuing himself. He was George C. Griscom, Jr., a plump, sideburned forty-two-year-old who lived with his elderly parents in Pittsburgh, and summered at Nantucket. Griscom urged all whom he met to call him 'Junior.' When his parents traveled, he invariably accompanied them. One report said his doting mother still bought all his shirts and ties. Even so, Junior had his moments of independence and so, it appeared, did Dorothy. Soon the newspapers revealed that she and Griscom, whom she presumably met while at Bryn Mawr, had at one time called themselves engaged. After this came a real shocker: recently the two had spent a week together in Boston! During the summer of 1910 Dorothy had dutifully gone with her family to their summer home at York Harbor, Maine. Then, in mid-September, she had asked her parents if she might spend a week in Cambridge with a former college classmate named Theodora Bates. Her parents extended permission, and on September 16 Dorothy departed. But she did not go to Cambridge. Instead, she stayed in Boston, where she was met by Junior Griscom, who had arrived the day before and registered at the Hotel Essex. On the morning of Dorothy's arrival Junior had gone to the Hotel Lenox, where he reserved a room and bath for her. During the following week, the two were seen together constantly. Looking animated and happy, they made no effort to hide their identities or their presence in Boston. At the Lenox, Dorothy registered under her real name, with the correct New York address. Two days before leaving Boston, she visited a pawnshop on Boylston Street, obtaining $60 for $500 worth of assorted personal jewelry. Again she used her right name and address. It was the sharp-eyed pawnbroker who exploded to the press and police the story of her Boston sojourn.

Nothing titillates public curiosity like a lie discovered, and the press cashed in on the revelation about Arnold's time in Boston. The *Washington Post* reported on January 31, "This was an abrupt change, from the statements given out by Arnold and the lawyers on Saturday, when they asserted that he had gone to Europe on December 3. ... There was a strong idea yesterday that Mrs. Arnold had left home because of word that had reached her from Miss Dorothy Arnold, and that the trip of John W. Arnold to Europe had the double purpose in view of getting some clue to the whereabouts of his mother and sister. In a talk with the American on Saturday, Miss Marjorie Arnold, sister of the missing heiress, said she did not know where her mother had gone. It was all a mystery to her. Lawyer Keith insisted yesterday that Miss Marjorie Arnold was mistaken; that the lady did know where she was, but that her hiding place was being kept secret because it was desirable to keep her away from the turmoil that had come upon the publication of the disappearance of her daughter. 'I will not tell where Mrs. Arnold is,' declared Mr. Keith."

Irritated that they might have spent a great deal of money and manpower on a wild goose chase, the police closed in on the family attorney, who apparently kept his cool under pressure. "Mr. Keith was interrogated concerning the persistent reports that there had been a quarrel in the Arnold family, and that Mrs. Arnold's sympathies lay with her daughter. 'Oh, that is all nonsense,' he declared, 'The Arnold family got along as well as any other family. The father and mother have been devoted to each other. The daughter, Miss Dorothy, was fond of her father and mother.'"

In an unusual journalistic tactic, the author of the article saved what was perhaps the most provocative news for the middle of the story, telling readers, "On his return from Europe John W. Arnold, surrounded by newspaper men, declared that he did not know his mother had left home. He assumed ignorance of the disappearance of his sister until he was told that the newspapers had been printing the fact for three days. When Arnold made these statements he had not had a chance to talk with the lawyers. After consulting with the attorneys, Arnold told of having got word by cablegram from his father January 20, telling of the vanishing of his sister. Then he switched this to say that he had heard of it on January 3. It was only when Lawyer Keith saw that the family had been placed in the position of giving out amazingly contradictory statements of the trip to Europe of John Arnold that the lawyer decided yesterday to straighten the tangle out. Mr. Keith told the American that John Arnold had given misleading statements because he did not know what had been revealed by the lawyers. He went on then to tell of Arnold having left the city on January 3, which flatly contradicted the assertion of Arnold that he had received word from his father in Europe that day of the disappearance of Miss Dorothy. I developed, from what Mr. Keith said, that Arnold had actually departed from the city with full knowledge of the disappearance of his sister. Mr. Keith laid stress upon the point that John Arnold, in leaving for Europe, did not have as his purpose the hunting down of George Griscom, Jr., the Pittsburgh man who had been courting Miss Dorothy Arnold."

As the article went on, Keith's words became even less believable. "While Mr. Keith insisted that Arnold did not intend seeking Griscom out, the lawyer did make it known that the family, previous to the departure of Arnold, had looked up Griscom in Florence, Italy, and had asked him if he could throw any light upon the disappearance of the missing girl. When Mr. Keith was asked if it was not a reasonable theory to suppose that Arnold had pursued Griscom in following up the investigation along that line already under way, he persisted that this was not so. Mr. Keith wanted it made perfectly plain, he told a reporter, that George Griscom had been entirely eliminated from the investigation over the disappearance of Miss Arnold. He was satisfied, he said, that Griscom, although previously an admirer of Miss Arnold, had no knowledge of her going away, and that he had played no part in it. The Arnold family, as Mr. Keith explained it, had come upon the possible clew that Griscom might know something of the disappearance of Miss Arnold through letters which had been written by Griscom to the girl. "It ought to be made plain," said Mr. Keith, who had arranged for the interview with a reporter at the Arnold home, "that Miss Arnold was not the sort of girl to have what might be called a romance. She was a sensible girl. She had possibly a dozen men who called upon her, but she did not lose her heart to any of them.""

A newspaper illustration of Griscom

The problem was that, while one could appreciate her family's desire to defend her honor, and by extension their own, their attempts to portray Dorothy as a sheltered, naïve maiden were hampered by the evidence, including the existence of her own P.O. box, as the article itself pointed out: "It came out besides today that Dorothy Arnold had been getting considerable mail through the general delivery at the post office for some time before she disappeared, and that a number of letters bore a foreign stamp and postmark. Lawyer Keith admitted today, for the first time, that Miss Arnold had been getting letters through the general delivery, and about which her father and mother knew nothing until after her correspondence was looked into. Mr. Keith, explained this by saying the general delivery letters were from magazine publishers, who had rejected stories and poems she had submitted to them. ... On the other hand, it was said at the post office that most of the mall handed to her through the general delivery window seemed to have come from abroad, so far as the clerks could remember. The last letter the clerks recalled having given to Miss Arnold was received about the time she disappeared."

While modern readers may either sigh over the loss of such intimate customer service or rail against the thought that Arnold's personal affairs were observed so closely and then reported, there was another reason why the post office remembered her specifically. The article explained, "There had been a particular reason for identifying Miss Arnold among the thousands of women who get general delivery letters. A little before Thanksgiving day she called at the post office and asked that her letters be forwarded to an address in Washington. She spent several days in that city with school friends." In other words, whatever mail she was receiving at that time was apparently too important to her to wait until her return to the city.

While the police were considering her a runaway spinster, her family insisted that she must have met with foul play and wanted all of Central Park thoroughly searched. However, according to the *Washington Post* article, the police were reluctant to do so: "Deputy Police Commissioner Flynn told Lawyer Keith...at police headquarters today that it wouldn't do any harm perhaps to make a careful search of Central Park for traces of Miss Arnold, such as a piece of jewelry or an article of clothing, but that private detectives might as well be employed in this business as the city detectives. Mr. Flynn, it is known, did not consider seriously Mr. Keith's suggestion that the park lakes be dragged for the girl's body. He told Mr. Keith that if the family were serious in that notion, that, of course, the police would help. The family did not go to the park authorities for permission to drag the lakes. Police Capt. Carson, who is in charge of the park station, said it was ridiculous to assume that Miss Arnold's body was in one of the lakes because the lakes had been frozen since days before the girl was missing."

By this time, police had turned their attention away from New York and toward another state altogether, as indicated by a newspaper story originating out of Philadelphia: "It was said at police headquarters here yesterday that Dorothy Arnold was until recently in Philadelphia, and had written to her father from this city. Francis Arnold, her father, and Captain of Detectives Souder, it is said, had a long distance telephone talk during which it is declared Mr. Arnold said he had received a letter from his missing daughter, postmarked Philadelphia. Captain Souder said he did not know the contents of the letter. 'I will deny anything published about the case,' said Capt Sauder. 'This story was given in confidence and I will not discuss it. I don't want any publicity given the affair.' Publicity at this time, he said, would tend to injure the work of those investigating the case. It is said Mr. Arnold may come to Philadelphia."

Thus, at the beginning of February 1911, it seemed Arnold's brother had gone to Europe, her father might be going to Philadelphia, and her mother, who was nowhere to be found, was believed to be in or headed to Europe. As a result, it's little wonder the writer observed, "As rapidly as theories concerning the mysterious disappearance of Dorothy Arnold were set forth they were broken down by the family and the lawyers representing them."

Looming over the entire case was the fact that it was beginning to seem as though Arnold herself had been leading some sort of double life, one as a dutiful daughter in New York and another as a daring renegade elsewhere.

Meanwhile, Lorenzo Armstrong, also one of their team of lawyers, insisted the story about her going to Boston with Griscom was untrue: "It is a cruel story, and there is not a word of truth in it. And I might say here that Miss Arnold did not receive any letters from Griscom through the general delivery. I am not saying, mind you, that she did not get any letters from him, because she did. A letter from Griscom came for her shortly after she disappeared. That was before Mrs. Arnold went abroad."

When asked by the press for the letter, Armstrong claimed "it contained only personal references and absolutely nothing that would throw any light on the case." However, there was more than just letters tying Arnold to Griscom; the press was all too happy to note the existence of photographs as well: "In answer to questions regarding a number of photographs of Miss Arnold taken by William P. Earle, of this city, a brother of Ferdinand Pinney Earle, the artist, Mr. Armstrong said that one of them had been sent to Griscom. He did not know, however, that Marjorie Arnold had requested Mr. Earle not to give out any pictures other than those which the family had agreed upon. Among the various photographs there is one of Miss Arnold and Griscom together, and it was the one in particular which the family preferred not be published. Neither Mr. Armstrong nor Lawyer Keith were acquainted with these facts today, they said. The picture was referred to as a 'group picture.'"

The bottom line on February 2 was that no one knew where she was, or whether she was even alive: "There are still conflicting notions among the family and lawyers and detectives who have been working on the case as to whether the girl is alive or not; or if she is alive, whether she is in the country or abroad. Mr. Armstrong is positive that she is not on the other side, visiting a mythical uncle in Munich, or anybody else, and, moreover, he thinks she's dead." And yet, that same day, the *New York Times* reported, "It came out yesterday that Pinkerton detectives visited the Marriage License Bureau in the City Clerk's office, in the City Hall, about last Thanksgiving, and made inquiries concerning a Miss Dorothy Arnold. Edward Hart, the clerk in charge of the Marriage License Bureau, vouches for the correctness of this information, and for the fact that a thorough search was made for a record of this Miss Arnold's marriage license. The search was so thorough, he said yesterday, that it would have been impossible for any man of intelligence to have forgotten the incident. That the Miss Arnold of that search was Miss Dorothy Arnold, the missing daughter of Francis R. Arnold, head of the importing house of F. R. Arnold & Co., is denied by the latter's counsel, but Mr. Hart remembers the case because in December, a few days after Miss Arnold disappeared, Pinkerton men again called at his office and asked for information about her. It is known that Miss Arnold left New York last Thanksgiving. ... That she went to Washington is admitted by the legal representatives of the Arnolds, who still declare, however, that her trip to Washington was purely social and was taken with the knowledge of and permission of her family."

The *New York Times* article went on to quote Hart himself as saying, "The case of Miss Dorothy Arnold recalls to my mind that two Pinkerton detectives called at the Marriage License Bureau two or three days before Thanksgiving and asked permission to look up the records of the marriage licenses issued about that time. The name of the woman in the case was Dorothy Arnold. The name of the man was refused, and so we looked up all the Miss Arnolds who had married in New York since Jan. 1, 1910. We did not find any record of a license being issued to Miss Dorothy Arnold, and had one been issued it would have been impossible for us to have missed it. 'Can you fix the date that the license may have been issued?' I asked them, whereupon one of the detectives replied: 'Any time since the first of the year, but particularly very recently.' We issue several hundred licenses every day, so you can imagine what a job it was to look through ten months of records. At that time the detectives said that Miss Arnold might have been married any time within a year, and that was why we made so complete a search of the records."

In essence, the article implied her parents had been concerned for some time that she might have secretly gotten married, though why she would not have told them remained unexplained. Regardless, the family tried to deny the report, saying through Armstrong, "The story appearing in an afternoon newspaper, in which it is intimated that Miss Dorothy Arnold disappeared from her home about Thanksgiving and was gone several days is a direct, downright and inexcusable lie." The *New York Times* also reported that the Pinkerton Agency's search for a marriage license was in vain: "The Pinkertons again called at the Marriage License Bureau in December, and for a second time we tried to find a record of a license having been issued to a couple of whom Miss Arnold was the woman. There was no such record."

By this time, Armstrong was doing some backpedaling himself: "Inadvertently I said yesterday that Miss Dorothy might have received letters at the general delivery window of the Post Office from Mr. Griscom. I wish now to say that Miss Arnold did not receive any letters at the general delivery window from Mr. Griscom, so far as we know. She did receive some from him at her home address, one letter from him arriving after her disappearance. ... I think it was...received prior to Mrs. Arnold's and her son's departure for Europe early in January. ... It was just an ordinary, friendly letter. We...are positive that Miss Arnold did not go to Europe when she disappeared...."

Armstrong then reiterated his opinion that Arnold was dead, in spite of the fact that her family were still desperately searching for her and posting her photo and information about a reward in multiple port cities in Europe and South America.

Over time, more information came to light about Arnold's Thanksgiving trip, and Churchill later wrote about it: "Just before Thanksgiving, she again drew her former classmate, Theodora Bates, into the complicated web of her life, when she decided to visit her friend in Washington, D.C., where Theodora was teaching. Dorothy arrived at Theodora's home at 1820 Mintwood Place late Wednesday night. On Thanksgiving morning she expressed a desire to remain in bed. That same morning a bulky envelope was delivered for Dorothy. Here indeed is a riddle deep within a riddle; this was Thanksgiving Day, when businesses closed down and no daily mail was delivered. Dorothy may have requested the General Post Office in New York to forward her mail over the weekend, but it is unlikely that this would have been done with such exceptional dispatch even if she had left postage for special delivery. Nor did Dorothy ever speak of knowing anyone in Washington who might have brought the package to Theodora's door. Yet the package did arrive, and Theodora always maintained that it came by regular United States mail. On accepting the package at the door, Theodora jumped to a fast conclusion. She decided that it contained the rejected manuscript of Dorothy's second short story, 'Lotus Leaves.' Yet there is nothing to support this assumption. Dorothy, still lolling in bed, did not open the envelope or even comment on it, but tossed it aside indifferently. Theodora, although her curiosity was fully aroused, asked no questions for fear of hurting her friend's feelings. On Friday, Dorothy further astounded Theodora. She came downstairs for breakfast fully dressed for travel, and carrying her bag. 'Why, Dorothy,' Theodora exclaimed, 'it's only Friday and you were to stay until Monday.' Dorothy shook her head. 'Oh, no,' she said, 'I always planned to leave today.'"

Furthermore, there was more to the story about her brother's movements in Europe than what was initially reported. In fact, one of the most interesting details of the century old mystery came out in newspaper reports on February 4: "That John D. Arnold, elder brother of the missing Dorothy Arnold, beat George S. Griscom, Jr., in a Florence, Italy, Hotel, and that he took from Griscom several letters which Dorothy had written to him was confirmed by friends of the Arnold family. They said that Griscom had conducted an extended correspondence with the girl and that when the family found this out John Arnold was sent abroad to interview Griscom. When they met the fight followed. Attorneys for the family said today that, while they are sparing no expense to run down every clue brought to their attention, they are still absolutely in the dark regarding Dorothy's whereabouts."

Chapter 4: New Searches and New Theories

Even as Arnold's family remained fixated on Griscom, authorities had ruled out the idea that Arnold disappeared because of some sort of romantic liaison. As a result, the police and detectives were following other leads, as indicated by an article in the *Washington Post* at the end of January: "They exhausted that theory after painstaking investigation, so Mr. Garvan says, and had to take a [different] line. Perhaps, as was suggested to them, Miss Arnold, as other girls have done, ran away to escape the tedium of a comfortable existence. They thought the notion that she might have become bored over an unending course of theaters and tea parties and luncheons and dances and reading, and dropped it all suddenly to see more exciting phases of life, was worth investigating. They went back for years, and tried to remember if her literary predilections would give a clue. She dabbled at writing herself. Last Summer she submitted to the Cosmopolitan Magazine a 6,000-word story called 'Poinsettia Flames,' a love story. it was rejected by the Cosmopolitan and one other magazine. She was unable to get printed some verses which she called 'Lotus Leaves.' Her sister Marjorie thought that one of her stories had been printed, but she could not remember in what periodical. So this phase of the investigation came to nothing. There was no definite indication that she had left home because she was tired of the humdrum. And so the family and their friends, finding no traces of preparation for flight and seeing no reason to believe that Dorothy was unhappy over a love affair or in her home life, concluded that her disappearance was not voluntary."

Even so, there was one small clue that indicated Arnold could have been meeting a man somewhere. According to the same article, "This afternoon a young woman of refined appearance, whose description tallies at many points with that of Miss Arnold, tried to buy a suit of man's clothes from a water front dealer in unredeemed pawnbrokers' pledges, and inquired 'about ships, sailing for Europe from Hoboken.'"

There were several problems with this lead, though. The first was that Arnold had not, as best as anyone could tell, taken anything with her that was worth pawning, other than her hat, coat and muff, or perhaps some simple daytime jewelry. Had she intended to raise money, she had more valuable items that she could have taken with her. Furthermore, it was December in New York when she vanished, so it goes without saying that she would have been very uncomfortable without her outerwear. If she had pawned such items, it would have been an obvious act of desperation, not to buy a man's suit. Likewise, if she had fallen prey to a gold digger, as this clue suggests, he certainly would have instructed her to bring her most valuable items with her when the two ran away. On top of that, a woman as well traveled as Arnold would have known where to find information on shipping schedules and would likely have already booked passage if she was leaving the country. Even if she had desired to travel abroad for nefarious purposes, she likely could have arranged the trip with her family's limited knowledge of its purpose and then gone off and started her new secret life with her mystery lover once she arrived at her destination.

Based on those reasons, authorities ultimately dismissed the idea that Arnold had planned to travel, for romantic purposes or otherwise. As the *Washington Post* story conceded, "Mr. Garvan and Mr. Keith, directing an army of assistants, looked for her in the Hospitals, examined the records of the board of health in this and other cities, sent private detectives to Boston, Philadelphia, Washington, Baltimore, and other cities, but no clue to the girl's whereabouts has been found."

By the first week of February, a nationwide hunt was under way for the missing woman. Even a paper in Huntington, Indiana noted, "Circulars giving a description of Miss Dorothy H. C. Arnold, the daughter of a wealthy New Yorker who disappeared some time ago, were received this morning at police headquarters, the offer of a big reward for information leading to her location being a part of the big campaign carried on by police and private detective agencies in solving the mystery of her disappearance. The girl is described as twenty-five years old, height five feet four inches, weight 140 pounds, dark brown hair, grayish blue eyes, bright complexion, good color and rather pretty. She left her home December 12 and the story has received considerable press notice."

Around the same time, a paper in Philadelphia reported, "Local detectives are scouring this city for Miss Dorothy Arnold, the Bryn Mawr graduate, who disappeared from her home in New York a month ago. From information furnished the local authorities, considered the most reliable thus far offered, they are more than ever convinced that a thorough search here will reveal some trace of the missing girl. Following what they consider a strong clue, John W. Arnold, a brother of the girl, and John S. Keith, of the New York law firm of Garvan & Armstrong, are in the city. 'If I make public the nature of this information now,' said Mr. Keith, 'we may defeat our own purpose. I will say, however, that on the afternoon that Miss Arnold disappeared a limousine touring car stopped not far from her home. In it was an elderly woman. We have obtained an excellent description of her from reliable witnesses. She was heard to call to Miss Arnold as the latter was approaching her home. She exchanged a word or two with Miss Arnold and the latter then stepped quickly into the automobile, which was driven rapidly away. 'We have traced this car and expect to locate it either in or near this city soon.' From what could be learned today the detectives have under surveillance, among other places, a boarding house where a young woman said to resemble the missing girl has been seen."

Just when it seemed things couldn't get any zanier, Griscom himself also joined the search for Arnold in early February. As the *Syracuse Herald* noted on February 12, Griscom began telling people that he expected to hear from Arnold within days, and that he would marry her as soon as she resurfaced. In the very same article, however, Arnold's family continued to insist he was lying, and Dorothy's father again claimed she was dead.

According to Churchill in 1960, "During February, Griscom returned to America with his mother and father. In New York newspapers he inserted ads in the Personal columns signed Junior, which begged Dorothy to communicate with him. No word ever came. The nation's police, working along various theories of suicide, elopement, amnesia, and personal rebellion, found only dead ends. Reporters were no more successful. Once the headline DOROTHY ARNOLD FOUND spread across the newspapers of the country, but this turned out to be a hoax. But through all the furor Francis Arnold persisted in his stubborn assertion that Dorothy had been murdered in Central Park. Now, fifty years later, Dorothy's body has yet to float to the surface of a reservoir. Nor has it been found buried anywhere. There have been no deathbed confessions of identity; Dorothy has not reappeared from a life of shame. The girl who seemed to have everything has never come back in any shape or form."

Chapter 5: Subsequent Sightings, Stories, and Hoaxes

As is so often the case, the mystery attracted its fair share of thrill seekers, pranksters, and outright cons. On March 20, a report came from Muskogee, Oklahoma that read, "A woman who registered in a hotel here as Mrs. Winifred De Loach, and who said she had eloped from Washington D. C., asserted that she was Dorothy Arnold.... 'Yes, she is Dorothy Arnold,' said her husband. He added that he formerly lived in Atlanta. He has been employed here as an automobile demonstration. His wife afterwards said she was Miss Winifred Randolph of Baltimore, and was married in Washington a year ago."

It seems strange how often romance blooms in times of stress, but in some ways it's logical that two people sharing the same adversity can eventually be drawn together, and that is perhaps the best way to explain the following announcement carried in newspapers across the country on June 10: "Hinkley Arnold, brother of Dorothy Arnold, and Miss Mildred Culver, a chum of the missing girl, were married today. Only about 20 guests were present. The shadow of the family tragedy hung over the wedding, in the great care that was taken to maintain secrecy. The bridegroom averted his face from the small crowd about the door. Miss Culver, who followed a few minutes later, held her bouquet before her face and hurried up the steps. The bride took an active part in the search for the missing Dorothy, making several trips out of town to follow up clues."

On July 31, the papers once more picked up the story: "The search for Dorothy Arnold, who disappeared December 12 last, has taken her parents to Italy, where it was at one time supposed she had gone to meet George S. Griscom. Jr. to whom she had become engaged, though he was not approved of by the family. Mr. and Mrs. Francis R. Arnold, parents of the girl, sailed June 15 on the steamship Carpathia of the Cunard line for Genoa. Their names appeared on the sailing list simply as Mr. F. Arnold and Mrs. Arnold, and the fact they were on board escaped attention. George S. Griscom. Jr., and his parents, when sought for after the news of Dorothy's disappearance had become public, were found at Florence, Italy, and it is believed that the Arnolds are going straight to that city."

While Arnold's parents were still in Europe, other news emerged, with a mid-October article proclaiming, "Dorothy Arnold to Return in Few Days Says Sleuth on Case." The article claimed, "A positive statement to the effect that Dorothy Arnold, the missing New York girl, for trace of whom an international search was made, is alive and well and will soon return to her relatives, was made by Roger O'Mara, the detective who was retained by George Griscom, her fiancé, to fine her after she vanished. 'For a time I was baffled,' said Detective O'Mara, 'but I always had a feeling that she was alive and well. Now I have every reason to believe I was justified in that opinion.' 'Have you definite information?' was asked. 'I'm not prepared to say that today, I don't care to say any more than I have.' 'It is reported Miss Arnold has been in Pittsburgh right along,' O'Mara was informed. 'I can't say more about it now, I tell you,' he repeated. 'Let Miss Arnold rest and she will appear.' George Griscom is living with his father in the Hotel Kenmaur. 'I have nothing to say,' was the message he sent to newspaper men."

In the end, this proved to be but one of the many rumors that surrounded Arnold's disappearance, and as 1911 progressed, Dorothy's story finally began to fade from the front pages. However, it remained far from forgotten, and perhaps inevitably, the story was resurrected on the eve of the first anniversary of her disappearance. Newspapers quoted the family lawyer Keith as saying, "Since the morning of Dec. 12, 1910, when Miss Arnold left the home of her parents not one word has ever been received from her, nor have we or anyone else who aided in the worldwide search that was made ever been able to find a clue as to what became of her. You may say that since the day she went away the family has never been able to get the slightest trace of Miss Arnold, and they and I believe she is dead, for that is the only explanation that we can conceive of to account for her long absence."

Arnold's case slowly faded from memory in the months that followed, only to suddenly reappear on newspaper front pages again in April 1914. Bold headlines announced, "PORT OF MISSING WOMEN IS FOUND PRIVATE HOSPITAL Maternity Home in Pittsburgh Is Raided by Police When Physician Confesses Crime SAYS DOROTHY ARNOLD DIED THERE Famous Mystery of Missing Heiress May Be Solved in Coming Investigation THE VICTIMS WERE CREMATED Bodies of Miss Arnold and Others Who Did Not Recover Were Burned"

The story, which was carried across the nation, told readers, "Startling disclosures were expected today in the case of Dr. C. C. Meredith and associates, who were arrested in a raid on that physician's private maternity hospital at Bellevue, long known hereabouts as the 'house of mystery.' In the big isolated institution on a high bluff overlooking the murky Ohio, many women met gruesome fate, according to a confession ascribed to Dr. H. E. Hite, one of those under arrest and full credited by District Attorney R. H Jackson. The victims probably numbered score. There may have been more, according to Dr. Lutz. And among them, he said, was Dorothy Arnold, New York heiress, who disappear mysteriously in 1910. According to the alleged confession, several Pittsburgh physicians acted as 'feeders' for the hospital, sending to Meredith for illegal operations women who came to them. In a number of cases, when complication resulted and were followed by death, the remains of the victims were heartlessly consigned to the monster furnace in the basement, according to Lutz. Meredith was held today in $12,000 bail on charges of performing an illegal operation and larceny. Miss Lucy Orr, alias Lucy Dumas head nurse, and his alleged chief assistant, and Miss Mary Snyder, nurse, were also in custody. The specific charge against Meredith is that he performed an illegal operation upon Mrs. Myrtle Allison of Wilkinsburg, near here, a year ago."

Of course, the press was not interested in the other women; unfortunate victims who may have met their fates at the doctor's less-than-skillful hands. The real story was Arnold, and that is where the article led. "Sometime after sending Mrs. Allison to Dr. Meredith, Lutz asked Meredith where she was. He said Meredith, he declared, said she was dead. 'Well, doctor, don't you think this 'dangerous work?' Lutz claims to have asked Meredith. 'Well,' Lutz says he was told 'there was a certain party that came to me from. New York and was traced as far as my office. It was Dorothy Arnold.' When asked what had become of her, Meredith was said to-have motioned skyward with both hands, indicating, Lutz declares, that she had been cremated. Pressed for an answer as to the fate of Mrs. Allison, Meredith made similar gestures. Strange things were found by detectives searching the 'house of mystery' today. Among the belongings of Miss Orr, head nurse, was found red wig and a complete set of face colorings. In the closet was 'found a complete set of instruments. They were covered with a pile of old clothes. A secret path over, which patients were said to have been taken to the house was discovered. Ashes in the basement and earth in a stone walled pit will be examined for traces of bone dust and quicklime."

In the wake of this story, the *United Press* interviewed Keith, who had visited the facility sometime before the raid, and he told an interesting story: "I was first led to Pittsburgh by a letter from a prominent lawyer of that city. Writing to me as the attorney for the Arnold family while the search for Miss Arnold was still fresh, he declares a woman in a sanitarium near that city claimed to be Miss Arnold. I sent for Meredith and he came to see me. 'I want to go through your sanitarium, doctor,' I told him, after explaining who I was. 'You cannot do that,' he replied shortly. 'Well,' I said, 'I'll either go through quietly with you, Doctor, or I'll go through with the chief of police and every reporter in Pittsburgh.' That settled it. 'All right,' said he, 'We'll go.' I went through every room in the house. There were several women there but no Dorothy Arnold. Then I went down into the cellar, right around a big furnace which stood there-—there may have been two— but could find no trace of the girl I sought. I did not look in the furnace. After I had finished with the house I went through every outhouse on the place, even exploring a pigeon coop in which several birds were nestling. There was not a trace of Dorothy Arnold to be found anywhere. I am sure she was not there."

Obviously if what Lutz had said was true, Arnold could have been there at any time after her disappearance and since been long dead and burned. Still, Keith worked for the family, and the family insisted that such a thing could never have happened to their daughter. Another small article from New York noted, "Francis A. Arnold…denied here today any belief in the story told there of her death. 'I believe my daughter is dead.' said Arnold. 'I believe she died the day she disappeared or immediately, afterward. The one theory to which I always have leaned is that she was kidnapped and made away within a short time. I never received any clue leading to Pittsburgh and I do not believe a word of this story.'"

Unfortunately for Mr. Arnold and the rest of his reputation conscious family, professionals investigating the case believed otherwise, and that they had solved the missing girl's case. On April 13, the wire services reported, "District Attorney R. H. Jackson made it plain this afternoon that he was personally convinced that Dorothy Arnold died in the private maternity hospital conducted by Dr. C. C. Meredith at Bellevue, which was raided late yesterday by county officials and detectives. He declared that while it was obviously impossible to state definitely that further disclosures will establish the fact beyond doubt, he hoped and believed that they would. The evidence contained in an affidavit by Dr. H. E. Lutz…is only a part of the evidence in hand that the missing New York girl was a patient of Meredith's, Mr. Jackson said. Although he declined to give all the details, he went so far as to say that a physician of unquestioned standing in the city had given him valuable formation to support Lutz. 'Dr. Lutz has come through and told us everything.' said Mr. Jackson. 'We have evidence that Dorothy Arnold was traced right to the door of Meredith's downtown office in the Schmidt building. We have learned enough already to convince us that in this raid we have broken up one of the worst places in the country. it is too early yet to tell just be revealed about fate by the arrests.'"

In response to this announcement, the press also released further comments from Keith, in which he reiterated, "I was first led to Pittsburgh by a telephone call from a prominent lawyer of that city. He declared a woman there had informed him that a woman in a sanitarium near that city claimed to be Dorothy Arnold. Within an hour I was on the train. Arriving in Pittsburgh, I went to the office of my correspondent. 'Where is the woman who knows where Miss Arnold is?' I asked. 'Can you bring her here?' 'No,' was the reply, 'she cannot come here. She is a nurse in the Bellevue sanitarium—where Miss Arnold is —and you will have to go out to see her.' Then I was given directions as to how to reach the place, got two detectives from a local agency and started out by trolley. When we arrived at the designated street we got off the car and went up a winding road, almost impassable to vehicles, until we got behind the lonely big house on the hill. Seeing that I could not approximately [be] observed by its inmates and not desiring to give any alarm, I simply posted my two detectives, one on each side of the house and returned to Pittsburgh. Later I saw Dr. Meredith, who was reported to be connected with the institution, and told him what I had heard. This seemed to worry him a good deal and he accompanied me to the house. In the meantime the detectives saw no one resembling Dorothy Arnold leave the place. When we arrived at the house I went inside and saw the woman who had given my friend the information about Miss Arnold. I am sure Dorothy Arnold was not there. 'Well, Mr. Keith, are you satisfied now?' asked the doctor after we searched the place, and I answered 'Yes, surely Miss Arnold is not here.'"

Over time, the story again died down and the public at large became less interested in Dorothy's fate, but for her family, the ordeal would never end this side of the grave. On December 29, 1928, another loss in the Arnold family stirred up interest in the story again. The *Associated Press* reported, "The disappearance of Dorothy Arnold, comprises an important a chapter in the annals of police mysteries as that of Charles Ross in earlier years, and Frances St John Smith of recent memory. Hundreds of disappearances are reported yearly to the missing persons bureau of the police department and a large percentage of the persons sought are found, but now and then there is a disappearance which baffles the most brilliant minds, a disappearance so inexplicable and without reason that it seems the missing one must have suddenly dissolved into the elements. Such a disappearance was that of Dorothy Arnold, the indirect cause of her mother's death today. ... There was no known mystery in [Dorothy's] life, she had had no serious love affairs, there was no reason for anyone to feel enmity toward her. ... Clues by the hundred were run down and all found worthless. Central Park lake was dragged without avail."

Arnold's story made the front pages one final time in December 1935, as newspapers across the country, anxious perhaps for a story to distract their readers from the tough times of the Great Depression, recalled her story: "Harriet Camille Dorothy Arnold, Bryn Mawr college graduate and wealthy society girl, disappeared just 25 years ago this week—and police of the world are still engaged in an international hunt for her. New clues, cropping up a quarter of a century after America's most celebrated mystery case...have caused renewed investigation of the circumstances under which the beautiful Dorothy vanished while shopping among the fashionable crowds on Fifth Avenue, December 12, 1910."

It is interesting to note how the way in which the story was told evolved over the years. Arnold became a "wealthy society girl," as opposed to the aging spinster she was portrayed as in 1911. She is also reported to have disappeared "among the fashionable crowds on Fifth Avenue." The way in which the story was viewed in 1935 indicates the nation had matured but was also struggling with hard times and looking back to a bygone era of prosperity. World War I and economic struggles had driven Dorothy's story into the mists of the past, though it was still of interest to many, if as a diversion more than anything else. The article continued, "The case is still marked 'open' on the books of the missing persons bureau of the New York police department, despite reports to the contrary. And scarcely a week goes by without reports that the heiress has been found—all of them false, but increasing the belief she may be alive. A fortune awaits the man, woman or child who actually discovers Miss Arnold, who now would be 50 years old. While there is no official reward outstanding, her discoverer would reap a rich reward, for the Dorothy Arnold case is recognized as one of history's classics, and its solution would be one of the big stories of the year."

The article went on to review a number of theories behind Arnold's disappearance, including the unlikely one preferred by her family that she had been kidnapped by white slavers and either killed or spirited off to some distant land. There is no evidence of such an abduction, and the theory is more representative of the dark fears of Americans during the time than anything of actual substance. For one thing, it is unlikely that anyone looking for women to sell off would target shoppers on Fifth Avenue when such activities were far better pursued on the poorer side of town, where unsuspecting young women could be spirited off unnoticed. If someone had kidnapped Arnold, it almost certainly would have been to ransom her off to her wealthy family. It's even possible Arnold's family believed that was the motive behind her disappearance when they refused for so long to let the story out, but no ransom note ever arrived. Alternatively, if she had been killed by her kidnappers, her body would likely have been dumped somewhere, and with forensic science still in its infancy in 1910, Dorothy's captors would have had little to fear as long as they were careful.

In the end, it seems Arnold's family accepted that she had not been kidnapped; after all, as the 1935 article pointed out, "Dorothy's family spent nearly $500,000 in their search for her, covering every city in the United States and many in England, France, Germany, Spain, Italy and the Orient. George S. Griscom, to whom she was reported engaged, dedicated his life to solving the mystery—and failed." And by the 1920s, the official family line had changed, with Dorothy's relatives now claiming that she must have committed suicide. That assertion was parroted by an article in the *Milwaukee Sentinel* in December 1928, which quoted the family attorney Keith as saying, "Dorothy was a temperamental girl with an ambition to write stories. She had written two or three but no magazine would accept them. Finally in 1910 she began to write one which she described as her 'masterpiece.' Some time in November it was finished and sent to an editor who, we had reason to believe, would look on her work with favor. While the story was under consideration she went away to spend Thanksgiving with a friend in Washington, and while there the manuscript was returned. She said good-bye and left for New York immediately. In the days that followed the script's return she wrote to the friend who had promised his aid in marketing: 'It is useless. You can't break in unless you belong to the ring.'" At the same time, Keith acknowledged he was "as far from [the] solution as ever."

All the while, the story played out over time, taking on something of a life of its own, as the article noted, "And today, just as much as on December 12, 1910, the identity of the 'mystery man,' with whom she was corresponding through the general delivery department of the general post office, remains unknown. One of the strangest phases of the mystery revolves around the frequent reports that Miss Arnold has been seen in New York. Such reports began soon after her disappearance was reported to the police. It was said Miss Arnold had returned safely to her home, and that she was being hidden there by her family. Reporters searched the house, and found no clue. She was not there, and had not been there since she started out on her last known 'shopping tour.'"

Having given the background on the story, the writer took up the issue of a new development, one which had police and family members alike confused: "But within the last month, along Broadway, people have reported 'seeing Dorothy Arnold.' And in Kansas City, time after time, as well as in other Mid-West cities, there have been similar reports. The Kansas City 'appearance' led to the discovery of a strange fact—that a 'double' of Dorothy Arnold exists—a 'twin' of the same heights, weight and age, with the same birthmark, with the same types of teeth, and the same facial characteristics. The 'double' recently identified as such, is Mrs. Anna Miller, wife of a motion-picture projector operator. She lives in Kansas City and the investigator, on meeting her was astonished by her resemblance—even though many years have passed—to photographs of Dorothy Arnold. Mrs. Miller admits there are many strange coincidences in her life, which might lead investigators to believe she is really Dorothy Arnold herself. She left New

York on December 10, 1910 just as Dorothy Arnold vanished—an amazing coincidence to police officials. And she has a mole on her right leg, three inches above the knee—just as Dorothy Arnold did. More than that, she used to dress as Dorothy Arnold did—police questioning her in the belief they had found the missing girl—fancy dresses, a muff and a fur coat bearing the label of a Fifth avenue shop located near where Dorothy Arnold was last seen. The investigators believed for a long time she was Dorothy Arnold, gone into hiding for some reason they could not explain. But she finally convinced them that she was Anna Miller, and was allowed to go. Now, although she says she is tired of being mistaken for the missing heiress, her appearance in public inevitably leads to reports that Dorothy Arnold has been found."

Another 25 years passed before Churchill wrote his piece in 1960, and he may have put it best: "What, then, happened to her? Some believe that she may have slipped and fallen on the icy pavement, suffering a concussion that brought on amnesia. ... Others point out that the drugging and abducting of attractive girls was fairly common in 1910. ... More likely is the possibility that she contrived, or connived in, her own disappearance. ... Did the rejection of the first stories she ever submitted to a magazine, which coincided with her father's stern refusal to let her live in Greenwich Village, or to see more of the idle Griscom, plunge her into a mood of suicidal despair? ... But people who are about to destroy themselves usually seem depressed. Dorothy's steady good humor at home, her lively anticipation of her sister's debut, the banter with Gladys King outside Brentano's—all these indicate a normal state of mind, not a desire for self-destruction. What else, then? ... She may have become pregnant by Griscom. ... This may have led to contact with the underworld, and the pent-up Dorothy may have seized on this road to a new kind of life. Or she may have died on an abortionist's table. But if she did slip into another life, her insensitivity was colossal, for she could not have avoided reading in newspapers of the distress she was causing her family. 'It would be bad enough,' the stern Francis Arnold cried out once, 'if the daughter I loved so well [were] lying beside her grandmother in Greenwood Cemetery, but this suspense and uncertainty are a thousand times worse.'"

Online Resources

Other books about 20th century American history by Charles River Editors

Other books about Dorothy Arnold on Amazon

Bibliography

Gethard, Chris (2005). *Weird New York: Your Travel Guide to New York's Local Legends and Best Kept Secrets.*

Raybin Emert, Phyllis (1992). *Mysteries of People and Places.* Macmillan

Taylor, Troy. *Dead Men Do Tell Tales: Without a Trace, Mysterious Disappearances & Supernatural Vanishings* (2009).

Watkins, John Elfreth (1919). *Famous Mysteries: Curious and Fantastic Riddles of Human Life that Have Never Been Solved.*

Free Books by Charles River Editors

We have brand new titles available for free most days of the week. To see which of our titles are currently free, click on this link.

Discounted Books by Charles River Editors

We have titles at a discount price of just 99 cents everyday. To see which of our titles are currently 99 cents, click on this link.

CPSIA information can be obtained
at www.ICGtesting.com
Printed in the USA
LVHW082230230321
682287LV00016B/866